THE POLES IN AMERICA

The IN AMERICA *Series*

THE **POLES** IN AMERICA

JOSEPH A. WYTRWAL, Ph.D.

 *Published by*
Lerner Publications Company
Minneapolis, Minnesota

ACKNOWLEDGMENTS

The illustrations are reproduced through the courtesy of: p. 6, Reni Newsphoto Service; p. 7, Jan Bulhak; p. 8, Jan Jaroszynski; pp. 9, 10, 14, 16, 18, 35, 38, 40 (top left), 43, 44, 53 (bottom), Independent Picture Service; pp. 11, 13, 66, Central Press-Photo Agency, Warsaw; p. 12, British Museum; pp. 15, 61, 62, Yivo Institute for Jewish Research; p. 17, Sigmund H. Uminski; p. 20, National Park Service; pp. 21, 25, 33 (bottom), 34, 36, 42, 78 (top left), Library of Congress; p. 23, Sadowski Memorial Committee; pp. 26, 27, 28, 52, Kosciuszko Foundation; pp. 29 (bottom), 33 (top), Polish Roman Catholic Union; p. 30, Post Office Department, Division of Philately; p. 37, University of California, San Francisco Medical Center; p. 40 (top right), U.S. War Department General Staff Photo, National Archives; p. 40 (bottom left), South Caroliniana Library; p. 40 (bottom right), Massachusetts Institute of Technology; p. 45, Polish National Alliance of Brooklyn, New York; p. 46, *Polish Daily Zgoda*; pp. 47, 55, State Historical Society of Wisconsin; p. 48, Francis A. Cegielka, S.A.C., S.T.D.; p. 49, *The Eagle*, Orchard Lake, Michigan; p. 51, Museum of the City of New York; p. 53 (top), *Dictionary of American Portraits*, Dover Publications, Inc.; p. 54, New York Public Library; p. 57, Leopold Stokowski; p. 58, Geoffrey Landesman, Cleveland, Ohio; pp. 59, 60, Collectors Bookstore; p. 63, Francis S. Gabreski; p. 64 (left), U.S. Army; p. 64 (right), Sadowski family; p. 65, Helena Lopata; p. 67 (left), University of Colorado; p. 67 (right), Indiana University; p. 68, Columbia University; p. 69, U.S. Air Force Academy; p. 70 (top), Wellesley College; p. 70 (bottom), T. Sendzimir; p. 71, Christian Von Plessen; p. 72, Minnesota Orchestra; p. 74, Carl Wolf Studio; p. 76, Blair Matejczyk; p. 78 (top right), Office of Media Services; p. 78 (bottom), Office of the Senator; p. 80, Ruth Ziolkowski; p. 81, *Post Eagle*; p. 82 (left), St. Louis Cardinals; p. 82 (right), Boston Red Sox; p. 83 (top), Buffalo Bills; p. 83 (bottom left), Denver Broncos; p. 83 (bottom right), Detroit Lions. Cover photo of Ignace Jan Paderewski from a portrait by Tade Styka. It hangs in the Crucifixion-Resurrection at Forest Lawn Memorial-Park, Glendale where also is enshrined "The Crucifixion" painting by Jan Styka inspired by Paderewski.

The Library of Congress cataloged the
original printing of this title as follows:

Wytrwal, Joseph Anthony, 1924—
    The Poles in America [by] Joseph A. Wytrwal. Minneapolis,
Minn., Lerner Publications Co. [1969]

    84 p. illus., facsims., maps, ports. 24 cm. (The In America
Series)

    A history of the Poles in the New World from the settlement
of Jamestown through their participation in various wars to
their present day contribution to American life.

    1. Poles in the United States—Juvenile literature. [1. Poles
in the United States] I. Title.

E184.P7W92   917.3'09'749185   68-31506
ISBN 0-8225-0218-6   MARC
                                                                 AC

International Standard Book Number: 0-8225-0218-6 Library Edition
International Standard Book Number: 0-8225-1019-7 Paper Edition

Library of Congress Catalog Card Number: 68-31506

Fourth Printing 1974

...CONTENTS...

Baptism of Duke Mieszko in 966. The Polish Millenium commemorates the Catholic baptism of Mieszko, ruler of Poland from 962 to 992. He initiated the Christian conversion of Poland and placed the country under the Pope's protection. (*Painting by Max Ingrand, National Shrine of the Immaculate Conception, Washington, D.C.*)

The town of Wilno, on Poland's eastern border, was declared Russian territory at the Yalta Conference of 1945. At various times in the past, it has belonged to Lithuania, Poland, and Russia.

PART I

Poland: The Land of the White Eagle

Poland is one of the few countries with a national image strong enough to have survived political upheavals, wars, and four partitions. During a period of a thousand years enormous changes have taken place in the boundaries and the extent of the Polish state. Poland has been both the largest political unit on the European map and totally eliminated from the map after being absorbed by her powerful neighbors, Russia, Prussia, and Austria.

Poland's present size of approximately 120,400 square miles was determined by Great Britain, the United States, and the Soviet Union at the Yalta Conference held in 1945, shortly before the end of World War II. The Big Three, as these world powers were called, agreed that the Soviet Union should annex a belt of land from 50 to 150 miles wide along Poland's eastern border. This was approximately 20 percent of Poland as it was after the 1939 partition by Germany and the Soviet Union. To compensate Poland for this loss, however, Germany returned most of the Polish land east of the Oder and Neisse Rivers.

About the size of New Mexico, Poland is one of the largest countries in Europe. Poland is in the same latitude as England and extends about 360 miles south from the Baltic Sea and approximately 400 miles east of the Oder and Neisse Rivers. The territory of Poland is a plain which slopes gently to the northwest from the Carpathian Mountains to the shores of the Baltic Sea. Before World War II, Poland was predominantly (about 60 percent) an agricultural country; today Poland is only about 40 percent agricultural. The population is over 32 million. In contrast to the pre-war period, it is ethnically almost homogeneous.

The traditional Polish national symbol is a white eagle. The white eagle, crowned, on a red field became the Polish coat-of-arms, and except for the crown has been retained as the official symbol of the present state. The traditional colors, white and red, also have been retained in the national flag.

Polish farmers at work. Since World War II, agriculture has lost its dominant position in the Polish economy.

The partitions of Poland: 1772, 1793, 1795.

1772	1793	1795
TO RUSSIA	TO RUSSIA	TO RUSSIA
TO PRUSSIA	TO PRUSSIA (INCLUDED DANZIG)	TO PRUSSIA
TO AUSTRIA		TO AUSTRIA

The Poles form the westernmost branch of the Slavic group of people. They combine the features of the Nordic, Alpine, and Baltic groups, which means that many Poles are tall and have long faces, light hair, and blue or gray eyes.

One of the scattered Polish tribes living between the Oder and Vistula Rivers in the middle of the tenth century was the *Polanie* or dwellers of the plain. This group proved to be the strongest and politically best organized; they gave their name to the whole Polish nation.

Poland emerged from political obscurity in the tenth century. The first national dynasty originated with Piast, who was said to have been a peasant. The Piast dynasty governed the whole of Poland until 1370. Piast's grandson, Mieszko I, married Dabrowka, a Bohemian princess, in 965. Dabrowka was a Christian, and she introduced Christianity into Poland. The Roman Catholic religion brought Poland into the orbit of Rome.

Mieszko I (922-992) and his wife **Dabrowka.** Before his conversion to Christianity, Mieszko, who practiced polygamy, had seven wives.

The Jagiello dynasty (1386-1572) followed the Piast dynasty and introduced the eastern Slavs into Poland. The Jagiello rulers played a major role in building a federation which linked the Poles, Lithuanians, Ruthenians, Tartars, and White Russians. Their rule was characterized by a religious tolerance almost unknown in other parts of Europe. While the rest of Europe was torn by religious wars, Poland's Catholics, Protestants, Jews, and Orthodox Christians lived in relative peace and tranquility. In addition, Poland gave asylum to many Scottish and French Protestants, Jews, Germans, and gypsies, in spite of the Roman Catholic majority in the country. Favorable economic conditions paved the way for reforms and cultural developments, especially in literature, science, and the arts.

Casimir the Great (left) and **Ladislaus Jagiello.** Casimir ruled Poland from 1333 to 1370. Through peaceful negotiations, he repelled the invasions of the Teutonic Knights and the Turks. Jagiello, the grand duke of Lithuania, became king of Poland in 1386 when he married the Polish queen, Jadwiga. His marriage offer was accepted because he promised to convert Lithuania to Christianity.

Because there were no natural boundaries to separate the Polish Commonwealth from her neighbors, Poland often mediated between two empires and two cultures. In her early centuries she had to repel Mongol invasions from the east and battle against the incessant border raids of the Order of the Teutonic Knights from the west. Poland has also been the middle ground for confrontations between the rival religious faiths of Christianity and Islam. Repeatedly, Poland repulsed the assaults of Turks and Tartars. Poland won the thanks and friendship of the great powers when in 1683 she rescued Vienna from the Turks and checked the Moslem drive westward.

Polish stamp of 1933 commemorating the Battle of Vienna. King Jan Sobieski of Poland defeated the Turks when they invaded Vienna in September 1683. According to many historians, this victory preserved Christianity in Europe.

With the death of Sigismund II in 1572, the Jagiello dynasty ended. Thereafter, the kings of the Polish Commonwealth were chosen by the electors, an assembly of nobles and higher dignitaries of the Church. In the eighteenth century, Poland declined under the rule of the Saxon kings. Culture and learning reached their lowest level. The breakdown of the parliamentary system was brought about by the "Liberum Veto," which required that laws had to be passed unanimously. Financial mismanagement caused the reduction of the standing army. Religious intolerance was introduced by the Jesuits. Because of these problems and others, the

11

Polish Commonwealth could not resist the invasion and interference in Polish affairs by her neighbors — Prussia, Austria, and Russia. These three countries sought to gain more of Poland's territory for themselves. Their success was marked by the first partition of Poland in 1772. This partition, however, jarred the Polish people from their indifference and instilled them with a spirit of reform.

The reforms began under the last Polish king, Stanislaus Poniatowski (1732-1798). An official Ministry of Education was established which was the first of its kind. In addition, peasants were protected by law, religious tolerance was once again established, towns were given more privileges, and provisions for periodic reform were made. A new, progressive constitution was enacted by the Four-Year Parliament on May 3, 1791. It embodied many of the ideas of representative democratic government that were popular in America and France at the time. It was hoped that by reforming Poland's political structure, Poland would be revived. Unfortunately, these reforms appeared to be alarming to her neighbors, Russia and Prussia, and this resulted in the second partition of Poland in 1793.

Gillray cartoon of 1791. Catherine the Great of Russia worked to increase her power by preying on her weaker neighbors, Poland and Turkey. Often dissatisfied with her wars with Turkey, she was encouraged by the lands she gained through the partitions of Poland.

Polish commemorative stamp of 1930. Enraged by the third partition and infused with nationalism, the Poles rebelled unsuccessfully against the Russians in November 1830. The defeat forced approximately 7,000 Poles to take refuge in exile.

When the partition reduced Poland to the status of a protectorate, a national uprising, led by Thaddeus Kosciuszko, began in 1794. His initial successes were soon reversed and in spite of the many valiant attempts and struggles of men like him, Poland was finally overrun and consumed by Austria, Prussia, and Russia. This third partition of 1795 erased Poland from the map of Europe and forced the separate parts to live as three different political, constitutional, and economic regions. In spite of the partition, Poland continued to exist as a cultural entity. The Polish people clung to their native speech, their Catholic faith, and their land. After many hopeless attempts to regain independence, thousands of Poles took refuge in exile to escape repression.

Abroad these men continued to struggle as exiled revolutionaries. It was their hope and belief that they would eventually be able to return to a liberated Poland. In the meantime, they took part in democratic revolutions throughout the world from 1790 to 1871. Polish legions assisted the French during their revolution for "liberty, equality, fraternity." They assisted the Belgians in their fight for independence from The Netherlands in the 1830's. In fact, for a time, General Jan Skrzynecki was Commander-in-Chief of the Belgian forces that won independence for that country. Later he went on to organize the army of the young Belgian State.

Jozef Pilsudski (1867-1935) led a twentieth-century movement to free Poland from Russia. With Austrian support, he organized and commanded the anti-Russian Polish Legions of World War I. In 1918, he established an independent Polish republic and made himself head of the government.

Poles fought with the Hungarian armies struggling for their freedom from Austria. Another Pole, General Jozef Bem, commanded a group of Hungarians during the Hungarian Revolution of 1848-1849.

During World War I, Poland was the chief battleground of central Europe. Poles fought against Poles as they were drafted into the German (Prussian), Russian, and Austrian armies. However, these empires which had shared Poland were defeated, and in their own revolution of 1918, the Poles succeeded in regaining their independence. In 1918, the Polish Republic was established in Warsaw with Jozef Pilsudski as temporary chief of state. President Woodrow Wilson of the United States, along with the other allies, wanted to see a united Poland once again. The Treaty of Versailles left some of Poland's borders undefined. A suggested eastern boundary was not accepted by either Poland or Russia. Russian troops invaded Poland. With Allied help, the Poles checked Russia in an impressive battle. The dispute was finally settled in the Treaty of Riga in 1921.

During the 20 years of independence between the world wars, Poland made progress in the redistribution of land, and expanded her industries. But there was still much to be done when Poland

Auschwitz, a Nazi concentration camp located in southern Poland. Opened in June 1940, it became an extermination center in 1941 when four large gas chambers were installed. Over three million persons were annihilated in the camp. (*Courtesy, YIVO Institute for Jewish Research*)

was again invaded. World War II began when Nazi Germany marched into Poland on September 1, 1939. The German invasion was followed by the Russian invasion in the east and Poland's independence ended abruptly.

Between 1939 and 1949 Poland lost nearly a third of its population through death, expulsion, and repatriation. The Nazi policy of extermination eliminated six million Poles.

After World War II, as a result of the Big Three agreements, Poland was transplanted bodily westward, losing 75,000 square miles to Russia in the east and gaining half of that area from Germany in the west and north. A Polish Provisional Government of National Unity took control in 1945. It took office on June 28, 1945, and was recognized by the United States on July 5, 1945. Stanislaw Mikolajczyk was the principal non-Communist member of a largely Communist government. The Yalta agreement called for free elections. The elections of January 19, 1947, were, however, controlled by the Communist party, in violation of Yalta. The Communists then established a regime entirely under their domination. Mikolajczyk fled the country in October 1947. Thus Poland, in its restricted boundaries, became a Russian satellite under Communist rule.

In October 1956, following the 20th Soviet Party Congress in Moscow and the serious "bread and freedom" riots in Poznan in June, a shake-up in the Communist regime brought Wladyslaw Gomulka to power. Gomulka was a former head of the Polish Communist Party who had been ousted in 1948 and later imprisoned for refusing to support some of Stalin's policies. Although the Gomulka regime retained Communist economic and social aims, it has liberalized Polish internal life to some extent.

Poland in 1939 and 1945. At the beginning of World War II, Poland was divided between Germany and Russia. At the end of the war, Poland gained German lands but did not regain all of her Russian-owned territory.

Many historians believe that Polish explorer **Jan of Kolno** reached the American coast in 1476, 16 years before Columbus.

PART II

Explorers and Pioneers

1. *Early Explorations*

The exact date of the first Pole's arrival in America is cloaked in legend. The accounts of Polish immigration to America usually begin with the mention of Jan of Kolno (a town in Masovia, north central Poland). Jan was a Polish seafarer and explorer in the service of Christian, King of Denmark. He is said to have piloted a fleet of Danish ships which left Copenhagen in 1476, 16 years before Columbus. The small flotilla was commissioned by the king to sail westward in search of old Norse colonies in eastern Greenland and to discover a new route to East Asia. In 1476, the flotilla touched the coast of Labrador, and then sailed down to the mouth of the Delaware River. As they did not find either the Norse settlements or a new way to East Asia they returned to Denmark. On the return trip, Jan of Kolno died, which is why his discovery of Labrador did not gain much prominence.

A Pole named Francis Warnadowicz took the name of Francisco Fernandez when he settled in Cadiz, Spain. He was said to have been a member of Columbus's crew when he sailed to America in 1492. Although there is no proof of this, there was a Fernandez who was left at Hispaniola by Columbus. Fernandez was later killed by Indians and thus became the first European to claim this unrewarding distinction.

A celebrated Polish printer, Stanislaus Polonus, lived in Spain at the time of Columbus's voyage to America. Polonus printed several books which told of the discovery of America. Word of the New World was also received in Poland by merchants who engaged in trade throughout Europe, and by university scholars who communicated with scholars from other countries.

2. *Jamestown*

Although Poles immigrated to America from the earliest colonial times, there were never great numbers of them arriving at any one time. There were several reasons for this. In the 1600's, before the partitions, Poland was one of the largest countries in Europe. Thus people from other European countries migrated to Poland — notably Germans, Jews, Scots, Armenians, and Tartars. Furthermore, in the 1600's, the chief reason for immigration to America was the desire for religious freedom. This did not apply to the Poles, however, for they enjoyed considerable religious freedom at that time.

The colonization of Jamestown was an English commercial venture. Poles were among the first settlers of the community and worked to supply England with the lumber and wood products that she needed.

Poland was also engaged in a series of defensive wars with her neighbors. These wars distracted the attention and sapped the energy of many adventurous men who might have emigrated to America.

The Poles' first recorded appearance on the American continent was linked with the beginning of Virginia. In October 1608, when Captain Christopher Newport anchored his ships *Mary* and *Margaret* off the Jamestown shore of Virginia, he had several Poles with him. Actually, this was no accident. England's interest in establishing the London Company in Virginia was commercial. In the early seventeenth century, England was suffering from a lack of lumber and wood products. She had to import these products from other countries, one of which was Poland. The Poles who arrived in Jamestown were experts and instructors in the manufacture of glass, pitch, tar, and other products that England imported from Poland.

The Poles were hard workers. Immediately after arriving they started to dig wells, build shelters, clear the land, and cut down trees for the manufacture of wood products. On a tract of land allotted them about a mile from the fort, they also began to build a glass furnace. In the autumn of 1608, almost 12 years before the Pilgrims landed in Plymouth, the first factory in America was producing glass. Glass was part of the first cargo of exports. Later that year Captain John Smith wrote in a letter, "We sent home ample proof of Pitch, Tarre, Glass."

The skilled Polish pioneers proved to be such an asset to the first English colony that more of their countrymen were invited to settle in Jamestown. Within a few years, 50 Poles were living in Jamestown. Captain Smith's manuscript, *True Travels*, expresses his respect for and satisfaction with the Poles in his colony. Captain Smith recognized the Poles as fine craftsmen and good soldiers against hostile Indians. In 1609, when the Indians set an ambush to kill Captain Smith, the Poles saved his life and captured the Indian chief.

In 1608, the Poles at Jamestown built a glass furnace and began producing glass, thus establishing the first factory in America. The glasshouse has been restored and demonstrations of the early method are given daily.

As of 1619, only English citizens in Jamestown were allowed a voice in the government. The Poles protested this discrimination by staging a labor strike at the first Virginia Assembly meeting on July 30. The Poles refused to work until they were granted privileges equal to those of the English.

3. *Pioneers of American Liberty*

The Polish pioneers in Jamestown were also among the first champions of American civil liberties. In 1619, during the administration of Sir George Yeardley, the London Company gave the men of English descent in the Virginia colony the right to share in their own government. The Poles, however, were denied this privilege. Angry at this inequality, they staged a protest at the first Virginia Assembly on July 30, 1619. As a further protest, the Poles refused to work until they were given the same voting privileges as those enjoyed by the English settlers. They suspended operations in the glass factory, the tar distillery, and the soap factories.

Thus in the summer of 1619 the first popular assembly and the first labor walkout in America occurred. Governor Yeardley and the legislature were quick to correct this injustice. They realized that if the colony sent empty ships to England the consequences could be very unpleasant. Except for the few pounds of tobacco the English colonists were beginning to export, practically all of the profits realized by the London Company came from the resale of the products that the Polish-organized industries had produced. The governor gave the following account of the incident in the Virginia County Court Book:

> Upon some dispute of the Polonians resident in Virginia, it was now agreed (notwithstanding any former order to the contrary) that they shall be enfranchised and made as free as any inhabitant there whatsoever; and because their skill in making pitch and tar and soap ashes shall not die with them, it is agreed that some young men shall be put unto them to learn their skill and knowledge therein for the benefit of the country hereafter.

From the excerpt, it is evident that this first strike in America was conducted not for higher wages and better working conditions, but for democratic rights.

4. New Amsterdam

The Poles of New Amsterdam (now New York City) were considered a distinct asset to colonial life. Governor Peter Stuyvesant made every effort to induce them to settle in New Netherland so that they might help in farming and assist in the defense of the colony against the English.

Many Polish educators were also invited to the colony. Dr. Alexander Kurcyusz, known in American history as Dr. Alexander Curtius, is credited with founding the first institution of higher learning in New Amsterdam. He was also a prominent physician.

Other successful Poles who were citizens of New Amsterdam included several political figures. Captain Marcin Krygier served as co-Burgomaster of New Amsterdam in 1653 and again in 1654 and 1661. Krygier, one of Governor Stuyvesant's most trusted administrators, also commanded one of the town's forts, named "Casimir," the first Polish topographical name on the American continent.

In 1662, an exiled Polish nobleman, Olbracht Zaborowski (1638-1711), who claimed descent from King Jan Sobieski, settled in New Amsterdam and later acquired a large tract of land in New Jersey. In 1682 his estate extended from the Hudson River on the east to the Hackensack River on the west. Known as a trader, friend

Anthony Sadowski (1669-1736), trader and interpreter. *(By permission of Henry Archacki, the artist)*

of the Indians, and interpreter, Zaborowski also held positions of authority. He was the first justice of the peace for Upper Bergen County, New Jersey. The family name, slightly modified to Zabriskie, survives to this day among his descendants in New York and New Jersey.

5. *The Sadowski Family*

Among the Poles in colonial America were backwoodsmen who explored the remote and uninhabited wilderness in their quest for land and adventure. The most prominent Polish frontiersman was undoubtedly Anthony Sadowski (c. 1669-1736), who came to America in the first decade of the eighteenth century and settled briefly in New Jersey. In 1712, he bought 400 acres of land along the Schuylkill River in what is now Berks County, Pennsylvania. Within a short time, his talent for learning languages and his courage made him a natural Indian trader and interpreter. In 1728, Pennsylvania Governor Patrick Gordon employed him as an envoy to the Indians during negotiations to restore peace with the white settlers. When the Indians began crossing the Alleghenies in increasing numbers, Sadowski followed their trails down the Allegheny, Ohio, and other rivers so that he could continue trading with them.

When Anthony Sadowski died, his pioneering ventures were continued by his descendants, who became trailblazers in the Middle West. In the history of Kentucky, his grandsons, Jacob and James, are known as "long hunters, skilled Indian fighters, and traders." Jacob and James were members of Captain Thomas Bullitt's surveying party which laid out the present site of Louisville, Kentucky, in 1773. They returned to Kentucky with another surveying party under James Douglas in 1774. In May of that year, they camped on the site of the present city of Cincinnati and cut the first trees ever hewn upon that ground by white men. In 1774, Jacob was among the party of surveyors headed by James Harrod, who built Harrodsburg, the first permanent settlement in Kentucky. Jacob and several companions are said to have made a canoe voyage in which they reached New Orleans by the Cumberland, Ohio, and Mississippi rivers, the first white men from the English colonies to descend two of those rivers.

Emanuel and John Sadowski, brothers of Jacob and James, also shared the family spirit of adventure. Emanuel helped cut the first road to Tennessee and John served with a Virginia regiment during the American Revolution. He was captured during the battle of Charleston and died in a British prison camp.

Thaddeus Kosciuszko (1746-1817). Kosciuszko used his military background to fight with the Americans for independence.

PART III

Poles in the War for American Independence

Many Polish patriots fled their troubled country and joined the revolutions for independence and freedom in countries throughout the world. Most of these Poles preferred to go to nearby European countries so that they would be able to return to Poland when necessary. But, in spite of the distance to America, there were many idealistic Poles who came to fight for American independence. Thaddeus Kosciuszko and Count Casimir Pulaski were the most distinguished among these patriots.

Thaddeus Kosciuszko at West Point. During the Revolutionary War, Kosciuszko planned the fortification of West Point. Later, he suggested West Point as the location for the proposed training school for young men.

1. *Thaddeus Kosciuszko*

General Kosciuszko (1746-1817) presented himself to the Continental Congress in Philadelphia in 1776. His knowledge of military engineering was so impressive and his unwavering enthusiasm for freedom so great that he was appointed a colonel of engineers and assigned to the northern army. Kosciuszko organized the defenses of Ticonderoga, Mount Independence, and West Point. He also contributed to the decisive victory over General Burgoyne's forces by constructing defenses at Bemis Heights, near Saratoga. Kosciuszko's greatest service in aiding the American cause was in strengthening the fortifications at Saratoga, where the British surrendered to General Gates on October 17, 1777. This is generally considered the turning point of the American Revolution. It was after the defeat of the English at Saratoga that France agreed to conclude an alliance with the Americans.

When General Greene became commander of the southern army, Kosciuszko joined him as chief-of-engineers. For Kosciuszko's distinguished service to the cause of American independence, Congress awarded him American citizenship, a pension with landed estates in Franklin County, Ohio, and the rank of brigadier general.

Kosciuszko returned to Poland in 1784. Ten years later, he led an uprising to try to prevent the third partition of Poland. The attempt failed. Poland was divided among its three neighbors and Kosciuszko was jailed in Russia for two years.

Since America had just won her independence, she was especially sympathetic to Poland's situation. Editorials protesting Poland's seizure appeared in newspapers throughout America.

When the Russians released him from jail in 1797, Kosciuszko, who was now called the "hero of two worlds," returned to America. This time he planned to remain, but a secret mission in connection with securing Poland's independence caused him to return to Europe. On May 5, 1798, before his second departure, he drew up a will which he left with his friend Thomas Jefferson. His will is the best testimony to his humanitarian nature.

Thaddeus Kosciuszko in a St. Petersburg jail, 1794-1796.

Philadelphia citizens welcome General Kosciuszko, 1791. Men replaced horses and pulled Kosciuszko's carriage through the streets to his hotel.

I, Thaddeus Kosciuszko, being just on my departure from America, do hereby declare and direct that, should I make no other testamentary disposition of my property in the United States, I hereby authorize my friend Thomas Jefferson to employ the whole thereof in purchasing Negroes from among his own or any other and giving them liberty in my name; in having them instructed for their new condition in the duties of morality which may make them good neighbors, good fathers and mothers, husbands and wives, in their duty as citizens; teaching them to be defenders of their liberty and country, of the good order of society, and in whatsoever may make them happy and useful.

Before his death, Kosciuszko wrote *Manoeuvres of Horse Artillery.* This general system of instructions was used in the War of 1812.

2. *Casimir Pulaski*

An equally famous Polish-American patriot was Count Casimir
Pulaski (1748-1779). In Poland, Pulaski had participated in an unsuccessful revolt against Russia and had to flee the country for his
life. In France he met Benjamin Franklin, who wrote a letter of
introduction for him to General Washington. Pulaski had decided
to fight for American independence since the Polish cause seemed
lost.

He joined the American revolutionary forces as a volunteer and
eventually rose to command four regiments of cavalry. Later he re-
signed his command to organize a mixed body of light infantry
and cavalry with lances. The "Pulaski Legion," which became a
model for Lee's and Armand's legions, performed valuable service
in the southern campaign. Among the many Americans who served
in the Pulaski Legion was Henry "Light-Horse Harry" Lee, father
of Robert E. Lee.

Pulaski has been called the "Father of the American Cavalry."
It was by bold cavalry attacks that he saved Washington's army
from destruction at Brandywine, and Warren Tavern; and it was at

Casimir Pulaski leads his Legion in the defense of Savannah, 1779. During
this battle, Pulaski was fatally wounded.

the head of his own Legion that he marched in 1779 into South Carolina and lifted the impending siege of Charleston. In the defense of Savannah in 1779, Pulaski was mortally wounded; he died on board the ship *Wasp,* where he had been taken for treatment. Several months before his death he wrote the following note to Congress: "I could not submit to stoop before the sovereigns of Europe, so I came here to hazard all for the freedom of America."

In 1931, the United States Government issued a stamp commemorating the death of Pulaski.

Brave men served America throughout the Revolutionary War, but a special spirit had gone with the death of Pulaski. The Pulaski Legion was the "best cavalry the rebels ever had," wrote Major F. Skelly, brigade major of the English forces at Charleston. The losses of the Legion at the siege of Savannah were so great that it was disbanded. Casimir Pulaski is remembered not only for what he did, but also for what he stood for. Numerous memorials in the United States have been erected or named in his honor, including the "Pulaski Skyway," a $21-million elevated highway in northern New Jersey.

3. *Other Polish Patriots*

Kosciuszko and Pulaski were not the only Poles who made outstanding contributions to the American Revolution. Captain Felix Miklaszewicz was among the few foreigners who served America on the seas during the war. Miklaszewicz's privateering expeditions were so successful that he was able to purchase his own vessel, *Scotch Trick,* and send it to pursue the British in 1782. In 1783, he secured another vessel, christened *Prince Radziwill,* to cruise against the enemy.

Besides serving in the American Continental Army, in the militia, or by privateering, Poles served in the French army that was sent to America by King Louis XVI in 1780. The commander of the French army was General Armand Louis de Contaut Biron, Duke of Lauzun, and his corps is known in American history as the "Legion of Lauzun." Captain John Mieszkowski, who served under Biron, distinguished himself by exceptional bravery during the siege of Yorktown. For his services, Louis XVI sent him a commendatory letter and an award of 400 pounds.

Arms-bearing was not the only role Poles played in the war effort. It takes money as well as munitions to fight a war. Haym Salomon (1740-1785), a patriot and financier, came to America after taking part in an unsuccessful struggle for Polish independence. Salomon operated a brokerage house in Philadelphia and aided merchant Robert Morris, known as "financier of the American Revolution," in securing loans and money to finance the war. He loaned or gave to the Revolutionary government $658,007.43. When Haym Salomon died in 1785 his family was left practically penniless, while the government owed his estate as much as $350,000, none of which was ever repaid.

PART IV

Polish-Americans: 1783-1865

With the end of the Revolutionary War, a relatively small but continuous migration of Poles came to America. These Poles were political exiles — either military men by profession or members of the upper classes. Although Poland had undergone a third partition which divided her among her three neighbors, the Polish people did not lose hope for a reunited Poland. As a result, there were numerous attempted insurrections. When these failed, the participants had to flee the land for fear of imprisonment or death. Other Poles chose emigration in preference to living in a defeated Poland as a subject of either Russia, Austria, or Prussia. The Polish-Americans shed their blood in every major American conflict of the period: the War of 1812, the Florida campaign against the Seminoles, the liberation of Texas, and the War with Mexico.

1. *Military Men*

The most distinguished Polish-American military men of this period were Lieutenant Felix A. Wardzinski and Captain Charles Radziminski. Wardzinski was credited with the capture of Santa Anna during the Texas campaign of 1836. He was honored along with Sam Houston and Stephen Austin during the Texas Centennial. Radziminski fought in the Mexican War in 1846. Afterward, he was secretary of the commission that surveyed the new boundary between the United States and Mexico.

In 1836 **Felix Wardzinski** fought at San Jacinto, where he helped capture General Santa Anna. He also fought in the Mexican War of 1846.

2. Writers and Artists

Many of the Poles who came made significant contributions in other fields. One of the most prominent Polish literary men to visit the United States was Julian Ursyn Niemcewicz (1758-1841). He was a personal aide and friend of General Kosciuszko as well as a celebrated poet. During his stay in America, from 1796 to 1804, he made an extended tour of the country, which he described in his writings. Niemcewicz also wrote one of the first original European biographies of George Washington on a return visit to Poland.

Henry Dmochowski-Sanders (1810-1863) sculptured many medals and statuettes of important pre-Civil War figures.

Paul Sobolewski (1818-1884) founded the first Polish monthly in the English language.

Other Poles contributed to the development and appreciation of the fine arts. Adam Kurek was a talented musician who introduced wind instruments into American orchestras and organized traveling bands. He is often referred to as the "Father of the touring brass band in America." Henry Dmochowski-Sanders (1810-1863) was a sculptor whose busts of Thaddeus Kosciuszko and Casimir Pulaski are still in the United States Capitol.

3. *Periodicals and Fraternal Organizations*

The second wave of pro-Polish sympathies occurred throughout America as a result of the unsuccessful Polish November Insurrection of 1830-1831. A Polish-American Commission was formed in Paris to help exiled Poles. Many prominent Americans were members of this commission: James Fennimore Cooper, the novelist; Dr. Samuel Gridley Howe, philanthropist and educator; Samuel Morse, inventor of the telegraph; and the poet, Ralph Waldo Emerson. Money was raised for the Polish revolutionaries and Howe was supposed to take it to Poland, but he was arrested on the way.

It was not long before the new Polish immigrants were a large enough group to deal with their own problems. The year 1842 marks the organization of the first important fraternal group, the

Association of Poles in America, and the founding of the first Polish monthly in the English language, *Poland — Historical, Literary, Monumental and Picturesque.* This journal was founded by Paul Sobolewski (1818-1884) and Eustace Wyszynski. The first Polish weekly in America, *Echo z Polski* (Echo from Poland), was started around 1863; it was edited by R. J. Jaworowski. Another important fraternal organization that was formed in the mid-nineteenth century was The Democratic Society of Polish Exiles.

DIALOGUES,

TO FACILITATE THE ACQUISITION

OF THE

ENGLISH LANGUAGE,

BY THE POLISH EMIGRANTS.

ROZMOWY,

DO ULATWIENIA NAUKI

JENZYKA ANGIELSKIEGO,

DLA

EMIGRANTOW POLSKICH.

Title page of Martin Rosienkiewicz's English language handbook, 1834. The book was printed in Philadelphia for the first Polish school in America.

4. *Educators*

Equally significant was the Polish contribution to American education. In connection with the first public school, Martin Rosienkiewicz wrote the first Polish book printed in America (1834). It was an English language handbook entitled *Dialogues to Facilitate the Acquisition of the English Language by the Polish Emigrants.* Colonel Artur Grabowski was commandant of the Pennsylvania Military College and of the Worcester Highland Military Academy; superintendent of the Haskell Institute at Lawrence, Kansas; president of Defiance College in Ohio; and principal of the Summerville Academy of Georgia.

In 1873, President Ulysses Grant named **Leopold J. Boeck** American Commissioner to the Universal Exposition at Vienna.

In addition, many schools and colleges were founded by Poles. Reverend John J. Lehmanowski founded German-English primary schools for children of German immigrants in Cincinnati, Ohio, and New Orleans, Louisiana. In connection with the movement to foster higher education, he was active in establishing a college at Hillsboro, Illinois, which was later transferred to Springfield, Illinois, and named Illinois State University. Leopold J. Boeck (1823-1896) founded the Polytechnic Institute in New York. Later he taught at the University of Virginia.

As a result of the political situation in Poland in the nineteenth century, there were a group of prominent Polish Catholic educators who emigrated to America. One of the most important of these men was Father Francis Dzierozynski (1779-1850). His work is an example of the fine contribution made to American Catholic education by Polish churchmen. He arrived in 1821 and in 1823 he was made Superior of the Jesuits in America, then organized under the title of the Mission of Maryland. He saved the Mission by solving its financial problems and expanding its sphere of influence. In addition, he founded the College of St. John in Frederick, Maryland, and was appointed head of Holy Cross College in Worcester, Massachusetts.

5. *Pioneers*

There were also many Polish-Americans who were interested in adventure and travel. When Alaska was a Russian colony, Poles had emigrated to Alaska and down to California. The gold rush of 1849 brought many more Poles to that state. Dr. Felix Paul Wierzbicki (1815-1860) was a famous California pioneer. After his active participation in the Mexican War, he practiced medicine in California and wrote a book on life there. Dr. Wierzbicki founded the first medical society of San Francisco.

Dr. Felix Wierzbicki (1815-1860). His book *California As It Is* was the first English book printed west of the Rocky Mountains. He also published the first California paper concerning the history of medicine. (*Detail from Bernard Zakheim's mural in Toland Hall, University of California, San Francisco Medical Center*)

6. *Abolitionists*

Poles were opposed to suppression of individual liberty because of their experiences with foreign governments who had ruled Poland. Therefore, many Polish-Americans became active in the abolition movement to oppose slavery. Those who were writers

Count Adam Gurowski (1805-1866)

expressed their opposition to slavery in their works. Julian Juzurkiewicz (1804-1839), editor of *Polacy w Ameryce*, spoke of slavery as the only deformity of America's social institutions. T. Lewinski edited the abolitionist paper *The True American*, which was begun by Cassius M. Clay in 1845. Count Adam Gurowski (1805-1866) was an educator, jurist, and historian. In 1860 he wrote *Slavery in History*, and his published diary strongly defended Negro emancipation.

Polish women were also active in the abolition movement. One of the most famous was Ernestine Potowski-Rose. An outstanding orator, she addressed anti-slavery groups throughout America. Dr. Marie Elizabeth Zakrzewska (1829-1890), a pioneer in medicine, was active in the movements for women's sufferage and the abolition of slavery. She founded the New York Infirmary and the New England Hospital for Women and Children. In addition, Dr. Zakrzewska began the movement to establish playgrounds for children in cities. As head of the New England Hospital, Dr. Zakrzewska had a chance to serve the abolition movement as well as the medical profession. One of the earliest Negro women doctors, Caroline V. Still, did her internship at this hospital.

PART V

The American Civil War

In 1861, when the Civil War broke out, there were 30,000 Poles in the United States. The majority of them lived in the northern states (the Union), although some lived in the Confederacy. Generally, the Poles did not approve of slavery. But they were so much a part of the life in their particular section of the country that they fought for the honor of their area, whether it was North or South.

The contribution of the Poles to the war effort was far greater than their numbers would have suggested. There were 4,000 Polish soldiers in the Union Army, including 166 commissioned officers of whom three were brigadier generals and four were colonels. The Confederate Army had 1,000 Polish-American soldiers and 40 officers. Many of these Polish-Americans were soldiers who had gained valuable experience in the battles for Polish independence. There were significant numbers of Poles who organized entire companies soon after the first call to arms. Two Polish soldiers received Congressional Medals of Honor.

One of those who helped make the war more vivid to the American people was the artist Max Rosenthal. He followed the army during the first years of war, making color lithographs of the camps. These prints were widely copied in the press.

Women as well as men were important in the war effort. In the North, Sister Mary Veronica Klimkiewicz of the Sisters of Mercy worked tirelessly to help the soldiers in the military hospitals. Although she was not in the armed services, when she died she was buried with military honors. In the South, the Barhamville Institute on the outskirts of Columbia, South Carolina, was run by Madame Sophie Sosnowski. During vacations, Madame Sosnowski and her daughters made frequent trips to Virginia hospitals to care for wounded soldiers.

Colonel Valerian Sulakowski of the Confederate Army (left) and **Brigadier General Albin Francis Schoepf** of the Union Army. Both had led forces in the 1848 Hungarian Revolt against Austria.

Madame Sophie Sosnowski, head of Barhamville Institute. Her students made bandages for wounded Confederate soldiers.

Edmund L. Zalinski, inventor of war equipment. Zalinski taught military science at the Massachusetts Institute of Technology from 1873 to 1876.

The most prominent Confederate officer was Major Gaspard Tochman (1797-1882). When war became a certainty, Tochman offered his services to the new government at Montgomery, Alabama. He proposed a plan to raise 10 or 20 companies to form a Polish brigade made up of immigrants who would enlist for the duration of the war. His plan was accepted. In less than six weeks, Tochman recruited 1,415 foreigners as well as 285 Americans, whom he organized into 20 companies. However, when the recruitment was completed, the President of the Confederacy, Jefferson Davis, refused to promote Tochman to brigadier general, a position that had been promised him by the Secretary of War. In anger, Tochman stopped his efforts to raise troops and withdrew from the service.

Before the end of the Civil War, numerous inventions had been patented by Poles. Perhaps the most significant inventor was Captain Edmund L. Gray Zalinski, who taught military science at the Massachusetts Institute of Technology. He invented the pneumatic dynamite-torpedo gun, an intrenching tool, a ramrod bayonet, a telescopic sight for artillery, and a system of range-and-position-finding for seacoast and artillery firing.

Polish immigrants receive vaccinations on board the steamship *Victoria,* 1881.

PART VI

Polish Immigration: 1865-1900

Prior to 1865, the Poles who emigrated were for the most part political exiles. Many were nobles and military leaders. However, after the Civil War and the California gold rush, America began to receive a new type of Polish immigrant — the peasant. Most of those who immigrated after 1865 were poor rural people who wanted to improve their economic situation. The peasants in Poland lived under terrible conditions, chiefly because they were part of a nation that had been conquered time after time.

During the last decades of the nineteenth century, Polish immigration to America increased sharply. In 1870, there were about 50,000 Poles; by 1875, only five years later, there were 200,000 Poles. In 1889, there were approximately 800,000 Poles living in the northeastern part of the United States. Even though most of these immigrants came from a rural economy, about two-thirds of them settled in the big cities. As early as 1880, Chicago, Buffalo, Detroit, Cleveland, Pittsburgh, and Milwaukee had become centers for Polish immigrants. Relatively few Poles settled in the South.

1. Work of the New Immigrant

Most of the Polish immigrants had to undergo a complete change in their work and way of life. Since the Poles came from a rural economy, they lacked both formal education, and industrial experience. Now they had to seek work in occupations common to a growing city. The phenomenal expansion of American industry and the introduction of additional mechanical devices and processes eliminated much of the need for industrial skill and experience. As a result, cheap, unskilled labor was necessary in industry. Poles worked as laborers in the sawmills, lumberyards, and woodworking establishments. They became stevedores, blacksmiths, bricklayers, carpenters, mechanics, and shoemakers. Poles were also employed in the garment trades of New York, Chicago, and Baltimore and in the New England textile centers of Fall River, New Bedford, and Lowell.

In the early automobile shops of Detroit, the Poles made up a significant part of the work force. Many of them learned English on the job or went to night schools. Henry Ford was particularly impressed with their hard work. He stated that "The suggestions

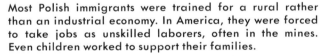

Most Polish immigrants were trained for a rural rather than an industrial economy. In America, they were forced to take jobs as unskilled laborers, often in the mines. Even children worked to support their families.

Poles learn English in the Ford shops, Detroit, Michigan.

[as to improvements] came from everywhere, [but] the Polish workmen seem to be the cleverest of all the foreigners in making them."

Thousands of Poles went to work in the great coal and iron fields of Pennsylvania, as well as the coal mines of Illinois, Michigan, Minnesota, Colorado, Arizona, Wyoming, Utah, and Montana. When the Poles first started mining they ran into some resistance from the Irish and Italians who already had established themselves as miners. However, it wasn't long before the Poles proved themselves as hard workers and equals.

Not all the Poles became miners or city laborers. About a third of them continued their rural life and remained farmers. Many of them established truck farms on Long Island and in New England.

Some Polish immigrants were able to use their background in agriculture. They often cultivated land that had been abandoned as unfit for farming.

Others reclaimed abandoned farms in the Connecticut Valley and specialized in onion and tobacco crops. By working hard, they advanced from poverty to prosperity and thrived on lands where others might have starved.

Some of the Polish workers managed to save enough money to go into business for themselves. Their earliest businesses were cigar and cigarette manufacturing, meat marketing, and baking.

The first board of directors of the Polish National Alliance of Brooklyn, New York, 1903. Fraternal organizations offered education, friendship, and news of Polish activity in America.

2. *Fraternal Organizations*

Homesickness and language barriers kept the Poles isolated as an ethnic group. Dissatisfied with existing leisure activities, they organized their own cultural and mutual aid societies, such as the Polish Roman Catholic Union (1873), The Polish National Alliance (1880), The Alliance of Poles (1895), the Polish Women's Alliance (1898), the Association of the Sons of Poland (1903), and the Polish National Union of America (1908). In the early days, these fraternal organizations conducted Americanization classes for the newest arrivals from Poland. They also published their own newspapers and journals.

At first the Polish-language newspapers were simply the organs of Polish religious, fraternal, and nationalistic groups. In style and format, they were modeled after European papers. Later, however, immigrant newspaper editors adopted a more popular style in order to make themselves understood by the uneducated majority of their readers.

The early papers were publications of opinion and doctrine. Gradually, they became similar in journalistic style to the American newspapers. To effect this change, the newspapers replaced lengthy columns with shorter news stories, and introduced advertisements, market reports, obituaries, sporting items, society and women's pages, and the inevitable classified ads. The exotic titles of dailies like *Ojczyzna* (The Fatherland), *Zgoda* (Harmony), *Pielgrzym Polski* (The Polish Pilgrim), and *Patryota* (The Patriot) only meant that these essentially American journals were published in the Polish language.

August 1968 issue of the *Polish Daily Zgoda*. Published since 1908, it continues to be printed in the Polish language.

St. Stanislaw Parish, Milwaukee, Wisconsin. In 1868, it housed the first Polish parochial school in the United States.

3. *Role of the Catholic Church*

The Poles were almost entirely Roman Catholic. In fact, their religion was so united with their culture that it became a way of life. Therefore, many of their social activities centered around their church.

The Poles organized a large number of Polish Roman Catholic parishes, schools, theological seminaries, religious congregations, publications, and church and civil organizations. The parishes, schools, and seminaries were staffed by Polish priests, teaching sisters, and writers who staunchly defended Polish Catholic culture and helped to keep the Polish language and traditions alive. For example, between 1870 and 1875 the number of Polish parishes increased from 10 to 50.

The first Polish parochial school in the United States was opened in 1868 in St. Stanislaw parish, Milwaukee, under the direction of the School Sisters of Notre Dame, a non-Polish sisterhood. Their one Polish member, Sister M. Thyta, was the first nun to teach in the Polish-American parochial school system. Soon another parochial school was started at Panna Maria, Texas, where the Sisters of Divine Providence, also non-Polish, served as teachers.

Mother Mary Angela Truszkowska (1825-1899) founded the Felician Sisters, the Congregation of the Sisters of St. Felix. The congregation grew out of an institute for orphaned children. The orphans often prayed before the shrine of St. Felix, believed to be the patron saint of children.

In 1874 the Felician Sisters came to America at the invitation of Reverend Joseph Dabrowski. The Felician Congregation was the first Polish sisterhood to teach in the parochial schools in the United States. The first Polish sisterhood founded in America appeared in Texas in 1875. Its members, recruited from Panna Maria and neighboring Polish settlements, were called Sisters of the Immaculate Conception. Within five years, they merged with the Sisters of the Divine Providence. In 1885, another order called the Sisters of the Holy Family of Nazareth laid their foundation in Chicago.

Father Joseph Dabrowski was a well-liked and influential member of the Polish Catholic hierarchy. In 1885, he laid the cornerstone of the Polish Seminary in Detroit. In 1910, the Seminary moved to Orchard Lake, Michigan, where it took over the site and buildings of the Michigan Military Academy.

This phenomenal parochial growth was not achieved without friction and difficulties. The efforts to create Polish religious institutions where Polish immigrants could feel at home with their familiar religious traditions was limited by the American Catholic hierarchy which was largely of Irish or German origin. Irish prelates John Ireland, James Gibbons and John Spalding regarded the use of the Polish language for church services, school instruction, and the press as un-American and also un-Catholic. These men were willing to sacrifice ethnic unity to the interests of religious expansion. They argued that all national differences among the Catholic membership should be ironed out by emphasizing Americanization and abandoning foreign customs. The unfortunate result was that Polish Catholics in the United States were not allowed to participate in decisions on matters within the Church that affected them.

Father Joseph Dabrowski founded the Polish Seminary in Orchard Lake, Michigan.

Consequently, many local controversies developed over the nationality of the priest, the language of worship, the nature of religious festivals to be observed, and the question of whether Church property would be owned by the Church hierarchy or by the members. Demands were made for greater autonomy for foreign language groups in the American Catholic Church, but these demands went unanswered. As a result, the Polish National Catholic Church of America developed outside the framework of American Catholicism. In 1897, Father Francis Hodur organized the first congregation of this new church in Scranton, Pennsylvania. The church adopted a charter which stated that its members, along with the priests, would share in the management of the church. Soon other congregations followed Father Hodur's example. In September 1904, 24 parishes (totaling 20,000 members) in five states formally united to form a new denomination. At this conference, Father Hodur was elected Bishop.

The success of the Polish National Catholic Church under Bishop Hodur forced the Pope to realize that the Irish and Germans were not the only national groups included in the Roman Catholic Church in America. In addition, the loss of 20,000 Catholics finally made Rome aware of the strength of the Polish Catholics in the United States.

To pacify the Polish-Americans and prevent further defections from the Roman Catholic Church, Father Paul Rhode was made auxiliary bishop of Chicago in 1908. He was the first American bishop of Polish descent. Six years later, Father Edward Kozlowski became auxiliary bishop of Milwaukee. Even today, however, the Polish contribution to the American Catholic Church has not been fully recognized.

4. *Polish Visitors to America*

Some highly educated and talented Poles visited America late in the nineteenth century. One of the most distinguished was Helena Modjeska (1844-1909), who first delighted American audi-

Helena Modjeska (1844-1909) as Ophelia in Shakespeare's *Hamlet,* 1892.

ences in 1877 with her performance in *Adrienne Lecouvreur* in San Francisco. Madame Modjeska was considered one of the greatest dramatic and Shakespearean actresses of the day, a reputation which continued throughout her American career of 28 years. She performed with other famous actors of her time, including Edwin Booth and Otis Skinner. In 1883, her portrayal of Nora in *A Doll's*

Marcella Sembrich Kochanska (1858-1935) made her operatic debut in 1877 before Greece's King George I and his court. In 1883, she was brought to America for the opening of the Metropolitan Opera House.

House marked the first American production of Henrik Ibsen, the great Norwegian playwright. Helena Modjeska gained such admiration and affection that her farewell testimonial in 1905 had to be held in the Metropolitan Opera House.

Another among those who have made significant contributions to American culture is Marcella Sembrich Kochanska. As a singer and as a teacher of voice, she represented the most splendid traditions of her art in both America and Europe. Marcella Kochanska made her American singing debut in 1883. Her repertory included a wide range of lyric and coloratura roles.

On the evening of November 17, 1891, Ignace Paderewski, a slim, nervous young man with pale skin and a shock of tawny reddish hair, strode on stage and played the first American concert of his career. Within a few months, the crowds were so large that Paderewski had to give his concerts in the newly built Carnegie Hall. Actually, Paderewski was the first solo artist to perform there. Altogether, he gave 117 recitals in 90 days during his American tour.

Paderewski was an active statesman as well as a brilliant pianist and composer. Several times in his life, during World Wars I and II, he interrupted his playing to work for the cause of Poland's independence. When Paderewski did play during these periods

Ignace Paderewski (1860-1941), concert pianist. "I owe my success in one per cent to my talent, in ten per cent to luck, and in ninety per cent to hard work. Work, work, and more work is the secret of success."

it was only to raise relief funds. He headed the Polish government briefly in 1919, and in 1939 he was elected president of the Polish Republic in exile. In 1940, he returned to the United States and settled in California. He died in New York City in 1941.

Henryk Sienkiewicz (1846-1916), the first Polish Nobel Prize winner for literature, traveled throughout America, as well as in Europe. His *Portrait of America* is a collection of letters about his stay. His most famous and widely translated work is *Quo Vadis?* In 1951, an American movie was made from this tale of early Christian Rome.

Henryk Sienkiewicz (1846-1916) won the Nobel prize for literature in 1905. The subjects of his books are semi-historical.

Cover of the first issue of *Free Poland*, September 1,
1914. It bears the white eagle, the traditional Polish
national symbol.

PART VII

The Early Twentieth Century

1. *World War I*

On April 6, 1917, when America entered World War I, Poland
was struggling for her freedom from Germany. Thus, the patriotic
feeling that swept the numerous Polish-American communities
had a twofold purpose: to support America, and to indirectly aid
Poland in her quest for independence.

During World War I, **Lieutenant Colonel F. Piasecki** formed and commanded companies of Polish-American soldiers.

American Poles immediately assured President Woodrow Wilson of their support and loyalty. Of the first 100,000 volunteers who responded immediately to President Wilson's initial call for volunteers, about 40,000 were Poles. The Polish Falcons proposed the organization of a Kosciuszko army of 100,000 men to fight as a special unit in the American armed forces. Within the first three months after the declaration of war, 38,000 trained Polish Falcons joined the United States Army. In the city of South Bend, Indiana, on the first day of recruiting, 94 of the first hundred volunteers were of Polish origin. Ignatius Werwinski, the leader of the Polish community in South Bend, received special recognition for his war contribution from the President.

In Milwaukee, Lieutenant Colonel F. Piasecki was placed in charge of recruiting men of Polish descent for the Fifth Wisconsin Infantry. In addition to Company K, he raised four other companies of Polish-Americans to form a battalion of the regiment. When the regiment was formed, Piasecki was promoted to colonel and given command.

Although the Polish population in the United States did not exceed 4 percent of the population, Americans of Polish descent accounted for 12 percent of those who lost their lives in World War I.

On the home front, Poles were enlisted in Liberty Loan drives, Red Cross campaigns, and labor activities calculated to promote the war effort. The publication *Free Poland* which first appeared on September 1, 1914, published the following front page announcement: "Do your bit! How? 1. Join the Army or Navy. 2. Join the Red Cross. 3. Buy a Liberty Bond." In fact, all the Polish-American newspapers and magazines beseeched their readers to "buy until it hurts." The response was enthusiastic. The same impelling forces which led American Polish youths to the recruiting centers, also led Polish-American workers to the Red Cross campaign centers and toward the Third Liberty Loan headquarters.

The victory in World War I and the independence of Poland had a double meaning for the American Polish community. The Poles had never stopped giving aid for the independence of Poland. Their pride in Poland's new found independence led to parades and huge mass meetings in many of America's big cities.

2. *American Literature*

Besides the monthlies like *Poland* and *Polonian Review,* some worthy books appeared during the interwar decades. Leocadia Popowska won the 1927 Harper Intercollegiate literary prize with her novelette, *The Living Sand,* while Monica Krawczyk wrote a prize novel, *No Man Alone.* Edmund Kowalewski wrote a volume of poetry entitled *Deaf Walls* and Alan Symanski wrote *Against Death in Spring.* In addition, valuable work in American Polish history was completed by Father Waclaw Kruszka, Dr. Karol Wachtl, S. Osada, and Miecislaus Haiman.

3. *Science*

An important factor in the promotion of Polish-American cultural relations was the stream of Polish scientists, writers, and artists who came to America during this period.

The noted biochemist Casimir Funk (1884-1967) came to the United States from Poland in 1915. Funk discovered vitamins and also coined the term *vitamines* — the "e" was dropped later. He stimulated public interest in the necessity of vitamins for good health, and discovered that such diseases as beri-beri, rickets, scurvy, and pellagra were due to vitamin deficiencies. In addition, Funk made major research contributions in the fields of sex hormones, hormone-vitamin balance, and cancer.

The anthropologist Bronislaw Malinowski (1884-1942) moved to the United States in 1933. Malinowski was noted for his studies of the primitive people of the Trobriand Islands (off New Guinea) and his theories of human culture. He taught at Yale and Cornell universities. His most noted works are *Crime and Custom in Savage Society, The Dynamics of Culture Change,* and *A Scientific Theory of Culture.* His books have been translated into French, German, Italian, and Spanish.

4. *Music*

Poland contributed two brilliant pianists to American audiences: Ignace Paderewski in 1891 and Artur Rubinstein in 1937. Rubinstein was born in Poland in 1889 and actually gave his first concert in America in 1906. However, it was not until his third American appearance in 1937 that he won great acclaim. Rubinstein

In 1940, conductor **Leopold Stokowski** organized the All-American Youth Orchestra and led it on tour through South America.

Conductor **Artur Rodzinski** (1894-1958)

became an American citizen in 1946. He still delights concert-goers with his superb performances and his delightful stage personality.

The American arts were further enriched by such great symphony conductors as Leopold Stokowski and Artur Rodzinski (1894-1958). Stokowski, of Polish-Irish descent, was born in London in 1882. He has conducted many of the important symphony orchestras in America, including the Philadelphia Orchestra (from 1912 to 1936), the NBC Symphony, the New York Philharmonic and the Houston Symphony. Today he conducts the American Symphony, which gives a series of concerts at Carnegie Hall in New York City each year. Artur Rodzinski's first position in America was as assistant conductor to Stokowski with the Philadelphia Orchestra. He also became head of the opera and orchestra department of the Curtis Institute in Philadelphia, which led to his innovation of presenting opera in concert form. In 1933, he developed the Cleveland Orchestra into one of the finest musical organizations in the United States. In 1937, he was selected by Arturo Toscanini to organize and train the NBC Symphony. In his long career he conducted many major orchestras, including those in Los Angeles, Chicago and New York.

5. *Movies and Theatre*

Many of the significant developments in the movie industry have involved Polish-Americans. Two of the best known names in the movie industry, Goldwyn and Warner, came from Poland. In 1918 the Warner Brothers (Harry, Albert, and Jack) moved to California where they soon became innovators in the film industry. They built their own studios and made pictures with money loaned by independent financiers. In 1927, the Warner Brothers produced *The Jazz Singer,* the first feature-length film with spoken dialogue. The Warner Brothers also contributed other firsts to the industry, including the first color newsreel in 1948. Samuel Goldwyn co-founded Metro-Goldwyn-Mayer Studios, but later became an independent producer. He developed a reputation within the industry for discovering writing and acting talent and also for his colorful misuse of language. Some of his well-known films include *The Best Years of Our Lives* (which won a 1947 Academy Award), *Guys and Dolls,* and *Porgy and Bess.*

Pola Negri, silent film star of the 1920's. During her career, she made as much as $300,000 dollars a picture.

Born in 1897 as Appolonia Chalupiec, Pola Negri became one of the best known actresses of silent films in the 1920's. Moviegoers thronged to see her in such films as *Forbidden Paradise* with Adolph Menjou. As a Hollywood star, she introduced painted toenails and dead-white face makeup.

Gilda Gray (1898-1959), whose real name was Maryanna Michalska, invented the shimmy in her teens when she was entertaining in Cudahy, Wisconsin. She left Cudahy to appear in the "Ziegfeld Follies," with Will Rogers, and in George White's "Scandals." Al Jolson tabbed her "Queen of the shimmy dancers." She went on to fame in the movies, and reportedly made more than 10 million dollars in 10 years.

Shimmy queen **Gilda Gray.** In the movie "Aloma of the South Seas," she created a mainland version of the Hawaiian hula.

Remains of the largest synagogue in Warsaw. It was destroyed during World War II when the Germans invaded Poland. (*Courtesy, YIVO Institute for Jewish Research*)

PART VIII

World War II and Beyond

1. *World War II*

On September 1, 1939, Germany invaded Poland in a well-coordinated aerial and ground attack, using what are often referred to as *blitzkrieg* tactics. This marked the beginning of the worst period of suffering in the history of Poland.

The Polish people fought with great tenacity—and they paid the price. More than one-fifth of the 1939 Polish population, which was 35 million, did not survive the war. They were virtually eliminated by the Nazis through executions, massacres, and starvation.

In spite of this, the Poles had an underground army that was the largest in occupied Europe by the time of the Warsaw uprising in 1944. Whole divisions of the German army, squadrons of the German air force, and other Nazi fighting forces had to be stationed in Poland even though they were needed on the Allied fronts.

Members of the Polish-American communities immediately condemned the actions of Nazi Germany. Many Polish-Americans felt so strongly about stopping Germany that they did not wait until the United States actually entered the war in order to fight. One of these men was Lieutenant Bronislaw Godlewski of Chicago who joined the Polish Air Force. For his bravery, Godlewski won three national decorations from Poland, Britain, and America. When the United States finally entered World War II in 1941, after the Japanese attack on Pearl Harbor, Americans of Polish descent were among the first to enlist in the United States Armed Forces. According to Army and Navy records, approximately 20 percent of the United States Armed Forces on the eve of World War II consisted of men of Polish extraction.

A German soldier leads Polish Jews to execution. Over one-fifth of the Polish population was eliminated by the Nazis. (*Courtesy, YIVO Institute for Jewish Research*)

Colonel Francis S. Gabreski won over 20 medals and decorations for his military participation in World War II and the Korean War.

Partly owing to the Kosciuszko-Pulaski tradition, Americans of Polish descent have for a long time been numerous and notable in the officers' corps of the United States Army. For example, five Polish-Americans attained the rank of general in World War II. Colonel Francis S. Gabreski of Oil City, Pennsylvania, shot down 31 German planes to become one of America's World War II air aces. Colonel Gabreski won 12 Distinguished Flying Crosses. He also flew jets in the Korean conflict.

Many Polish-American soldiers won recognition for their outstanding service and loyalty. William Grabiarz joined the Army as a volunteer in 1941 when he was only 18. He participated in five great battles in the Pacific. For his bravery he received nine distinctions including the nation's highest award, the Congressional Medal of Honor. Sergeant Joseph J. Sadowski of Perth Amboy, New Jersey, gave his life for his companions and was posthumously awarded the Congressional Medal of Honor.

World War II fighters **William Grabiarz** (left) and **Sergeant Joseph J. Sadowski**. Grabiarz was killed while using his body to shield that of a wounded officer.

2. *Community War Contributions*

The ways in which Americans of Polish ancestry contributed to the war effort were as numerous as the battlefields on which Polish-American soldiers have fought. In the Fourth and Fifth War Loan Drives in Chicago, Polish-Americans led all other purchasers. The Polish National Alliance and the Polish Roman Catholic Union purchased enough United States bonds to cover the cost of five bombers. These planes received Polish names, as did several other bombers during World War II.

In addition, the American Poles generously supported service organizations, and organized special committees to aid both war victims in Poland and Polish refugees. Through the American Relief for Poland, founded in 1939 and directed by F.X. Swietlik, American Poles contributed $10 million to alleviate suffering. Through the Polish Catholic League, organized in 1943 and headed by S.T. Kusper, they provided additional means for religious ministration to needy war victims. Finally, through the Polish American Congress established in 1944, American Poles financed additional relief activities and kept the cause of Polish freedom alive in America.

3. *Polish War Refugees*

Between 1939 and 1945 a number of well-educated and talented Poles found refuge in the United States. Among them was Professor Florian Znaniecki, who was visiting professor at Columbia University during the summer of 1939. To escape the war in Europe, he remained at Columbia as the Julius Beer Lecturer. Then in 1940 he joined the University of Illinois where he remained for 10 years until he retired. Professor Znaniecki served as president of the American Sociological Society in addition to writing articles and books in various languages.

In 1941, the versatile and talented musician Wanda Landowska (1879-1959) came to America and settled in Lakeville, Connecticut. She was an accomplished harpsichordist, pianist, and composer. At her new home in Connecticut she concentrated on recording her interpretation of the old masters. Her recording of the 48 preludes and fugues of Bach's *Well-Tempered Clavier* is a modern classic.

Sociologist **Florian Znaniecki**

Wanda Landowska in 1933. Landowska is largely responsible for the twentieth-century renaissance of the harpsichord and its music. She developed a technique of playing the instrument as well as proper interpretations of harpsichord music from the seventeenth and eighteenth centuries. Before coming to America in 1941, she taught and performed in Europe.

Many Polish-American scientists, along with other refugees and American scientists, worked on the development of the hydrogen bomb. Stanislaw Ulam, who was born in 1909 in Lwow, Poland, worked closely with Edward Teller and I. I. Rabi, two of the most noted men on this project.

Another atomic physicist who worked on the hydrogen bomb was Emil John Konopinski who was born in 1911 in Hamtramck, Michigan. According to Edward Teller, Konopinski proved by calculation that the H-bomb would not ignite the atmosphere of the world or the ocean. Konopinski also served as a consultant on the President's Scientific Advisory Committee.

Both **Stanislaw Ulam** (left) and **Emil John Konopinski** worked to develop the hydrogen bomb.

4. *Postwar Decades*

The decades after World War II were years of continuous progress and prosperity for Americans of Polish descent. More and more Polish-Americans became involved in charitable, educational, and community projects. Thousands of Polish-Americans returned from the battlefields to continue their education or resume careers. At the same time, the Polish communities received cultural transfusions from many directions. Displaced persons, refugees, and university students began arriving in increasing numbers. America provided them with opportunities for enriching as well as enjoying the land of their adoption.

5. *Education, Politics and Business*

Zbigniew Brzezinski, the son of a Polish diplomat who settled in Canada, has become one of the architects of United States foreign policy. Brzezinski was born in Warsaw, Poland in 1928 and came to America ten years later. Brzezinski gained his experience as a political scientist at the top universities in the country. After receiving his Ph.D. at Harvard, he joined Harvard's Russian Research Center and later its Center for International Affairs. During the administration of President Lyndon Johnson, he helped formulate new policies aimed at improving United States-Soviet relations. A consultant to the State Department, he is also a professor of law and government at Columbia University. Brzezinski has published numerous articles and books dealing with communism. He has proved that "America is a place where a man called Zbigniew Brzezinski can make a name for himself without even changing it."

Zbigniew Brzezinski,
scholar in Russian studies.

Another important Polish-American author and teacher was Dr. Waclaw Lednicki. In 1944, he joined the faculty of the University of California and for many years headed its department of Slavic languages and literatures. As the author of many books, essays, and articles on Russian literature, he acquired a reputation

Major George H. Janczewski

as one of the outstanding authorities in the field. Among Dr. Lednicki's 17 published books are *Life and Culture of Poland* (1944) and *Russia, Poland, the West* (1954). One of the more than 20 books that Dr. Lednicki edited was *Adam Mickiewicz in World Literature* (1956), a symposium on the Polish poet. In addition, Dr. Lednicki was one of the founders, in 1942, of the Polish Institute of Arts and Sciences in New York. He died on November 5, 1967.

Major George H. Janczewski, who took part in the 1944 Warsaw uprising, served as professor and Director of Research for the Foreign Language Department at the United States Air Force Academy. After emigrating to the United States in 1947, he worked as a reporter for the *Polish Daily News* in Detroit, and attended Wayne State University. In 1951, Janczewski was directly commissioned as an officer in the Air Force. Major Janczewski holds an M.A. degree in International Relations and a Ph.D. in Russian Studies, both from Georgetown University.

Waclaw Jedrzejewicz, a Polish army officer, diplomat, and cabinet member before World War II, is Professor Emeritus of Russian at Wellesley College. Jedrzejewicz also served as Director of the

Waclaw Jedrzejewicz, Professor Emeritus of Russian at Wellesley College.

Pilsudski Institute of America from 1943 to 1948 and has taught Slavic studies at Wellesley and Ripon Colleges.

Dr. Thaddeus Sendzimir, who came to the United States in 1939, revolutionized the steel industry with his new methods for rolling and pressing steel. For his achievements, he was awarded an honorary doctorate. Dr. Sendzimir lives in Waterbury, Connecticut, where his company's headquarters are also located. The T. Sendzimir Company has offices throughout the world.

Dr. Thaddeus Sendzimir developed new methods of processing steel.

Wieslaw S. Kuniczak's novel *The Thousand Hour Day* is about the Nazi invasion of Poland, August 24-October 9, 1939.

6. *Literature, Films and Music*

The contemporary Polish-American writer, Wieslaw S. Kuniczak, is best known for his award-winning novel, *The Thousand Hour Day* (1966). Kuniczak came to the United States in 1950 to continue his education. He received degrees from Alliance College and Columbia University. After serving in the Korean War, Kuniczak worked as a newspaper man and an advertising executive.

Bronislaw Kaper is a successful composer of musical scores for films. Born in Warsaw in 1902, Kaper wrote music for films produced in the major cities of Europe: Warsaw, Berlin, Vienna, London, and Paris. In Hollywood, he won an Oscar for his music for the film, *Lili*. The song from this film, "Hi Lili, Hi Lo", has been translated into 86 languages. Kaper wrote the music for many other films, including *The Brothers Karamazov*, *The Swan*, *The Red Badge of Courage*, *Green Dolphin Street*, *Mutiny on the Bounty*, and *Lord Jim*.

The conductor of the Minnesota Orchestra, Stanislaw Skrowaczewski, was born in Poland in 1923. Before taking his present position in 1960, Skrowaczewski served as conductor of the three major symphony orchestras in Poland: the Silesian State Philharmonic, the Krakow Philharmonic, and the National Philharmonic of Warsaw. In addition, Skrowaczewski has composed four symphonies.

Conductor **Stanislaw Skrowaczewski** of the Minnesota Orchestra, formerly called the Minneapolis Symphony Orchestra. His programs frequently stress modern rather than traditional pieces. He has been a guest conductor of orchestras all over the world.

PART IX

Recent Contributions to American Life

Between 1900 and 1925, nearly two million Poles arrived in America, and by the end of the Second World War, 140 thousand more had been admitted to the United States. Today, the American Poles number well over 10 million. If we were to include fourth and fifth generation Americans of Polish descent, the figure would stand somewhere around 15 million.

The greatest concentrations of American Poles are found in New York, New Jersey, Massachusetts, Ohio, Michigan, and Illinois. The American cities in the order of the greatest number of Polish-Americans are: Chicago, Detroit, Buffalo, Cleveland, Milwaukee, New York, Pittsburgh, and Philadelphia.

1. *Polish-American Religious Life*

The Poles in America, being primarily Catholic, center a great deal of their social life and education around their church. There are an estimated 800 Polish-American Catholic parishes, over 500 elementary schools, about 70 high schools, 6 colleges, 4 seminaries, about 35 hospitals, and over 140 other institutions. These establishments were built by and staffed with priests and nuns of Polish descent, who were supported by funds contributed by Catholics of Polish descent.

John Cardinal Krol, archbishop of Philadelphia. In 1967 Pope Paul VI appointed him a Cardinal of the Roman Catholic Church.

In the principal areas of Catholic population, Polish-Americans are often predominant in number. However, the numerical strength of the American Poles is not reflected in the ranks of the American Catholic hierarchy. Very few hold positions of importance in the American Catholic Church. There are only seven bishops and one archbishop of Polish descent. Most of these clergymen serve in the cities with large Polish concentrations — Milwaukee, Philadelphia, and Buffalo.

The Polish National Catholic Church, which broke off from the Catholic Church, has 140 churches in the United States. The membership in the Polish National Catholic Church in 1961 numbered 282,411.

Although most of the Poles in America are Catholics, many belong to the Jewish faith, and others are members of Protestant churches.

2. *Fraternal Organizations*

Today, Americans of Polish descent have approximately 10,000 fraternal, dramatic, literary, musical, social, cultural, religious, and athletic societies all over America. A good many are branches or affiliates of the Polish-American national organizations whose total membership exceeds 800,000. The largest Polish-American organization in the world is the *Polish National Alliance* with more than 325,000 members. It is the eighth largest fraternal organization in the United States.

The foremost organizations devoted to the perpetuation and growth of Polish culture are the Polish Institute of Arts and Sciences in America; the Polish-American Historical Association, which is devoted to research on the history of the Poles in America; the Jozef Pilsudski Institute, which is dedicated to research on the history of modern Poland; the Kosciuszko Foundation, which promotes exchange students between the United States and Poland, and also grants scholarships; the Paderewski Foundation, which makes grants to students and aids in the founding of chairs of Slavonic Studies in universities and colleges. The Polish Museum in Chicago collects Polish and Polish-American documents and materials for the use of future historians. The American Council of Polish Cultural Clubs, a central organization of 22 clubs, promotes various aspects of Polish culture.

3. *Alliance College*

In 1895, the Polish National Alliance established a scholarship fund for those who wanted to study Polish. This scholarship fund provided the basis for Alliance College in Cambridge Springs, Pennsylvania. In 1912, the college opened with its first class of 326 male students. It is now a fully accredited, co-educational institution with more than 600 students.

The Alliance College Kujawiaki gave its first performance in 1965. Each dancer is of Polish heritage. **Jan Sejda,** choreographer and director of the group, is an authority on Polish folk art and culture. In Poland, he choreographed, directed, and wrote for productions that involved 3,800 singers and dancers.

Alliance College developed a unique program of Slavic studies, which includes the language, history, literature, and folk arts of the Slavic world. A performing arts group was formed to give a living representation of the cultural heritage of Poland. This folk group, known as Kujawiaki, performs throughout the country. In 1966, the Kujawiaki group danced at the presidential staff's Christmas party.

Jan Sejda, who came to the United States in 1962, is the choreographer and director of the dance group. In his native Poland, Sejda studied ballet, theater arts, staging, history of dance, and choreography. He also traveled to Polish villages to gather material on local folk music and dances.

4. *Publications*

At the present time, there are five daily newspapers published in the Polish language in the United States: *Dziennik Polski* in Detroit, *Kuryer Polski* in Milwaukee, *Dziennik Zwiazkowy* and *Dziennik Chicagoski* in Chicago, and *Nowy Swiat* in New York. *Our Lady's Digest, Sodalis, Kronika Seraficka, Polish Review* and *Miesiecznik Franciszkanski* are but a few of the many journals, periodicals, and annuals published by the American Poles. At the present time, *Zgoda* is the most extensively circulated American Polish publication. More than 325,000 members of the Polish National Alliance receive it.

Endurance Press in Detroit, the Dabrowski Foundation in Orchard Lake, and the Alliance Printers and Publishers in Chicago are engaged either exclusively or chiefly in publishing journals of Polish or Polish-American interest.

5. *Politics*

When the Poles first came to America, they did not affiliate themselves with any political party. In 1918, Republican John Kleczka of Milwaukee was elected a United States Representative, a first in Polish-American history. Another Republican, Joseph Mruk, became mayor of Buffalo. Since the 1920's, however, the Poles have generally associated themselves with the Democratic party.

John Casinis Kleczka

John Gronouski

Edmund Muskie, Senator from Maine

One of the best known Polish-Americans active in government is John Gronouski. Born in 1919 in Wisconsin, Gronouski worked himself up through the ranks as a government employee. He was Commissioner of Taxation for Wisconsin from 1960 to 1963. For two years, from 1963 to 1965, Gronouski was Postmaster General in President Johnson's cabinet. He served as ambassador to Poland from 1965 until 1968.

Edmund Muskie, whose father changed the family name from Marciszewski, was born and received most of his education in Maine. In 1939, he earned a law degree at Cornell University, then served in the Navy during World War II. His political career began in the Maine House of Representatives, where he became the Democratic House floor leader. In 1954, he took office as Maine's first Democratic governor in 20 years. After two terms as a popular and progressive governor, he cracked Maine's Republican stronghold again in 1959 by becoming the first popularly elected Democratic United States Senator in the state's history. At the Democratic Convention in 1968, presidential candidate Hubert Humphrey chose Edmund Muskie as his running-mate. After the Democratic ticket was defeated in the November elections, Muskie returned to the Senate.

6. *The Arts*

Since 1948, the Boston-born stone sculptor, Korczak Ziolkowski, has been carving a monument of Indian Chief Crazy Horse and his pony out of the solid granite of Thunderhead Mountain, five miles north of Custer, South Dakota. Chief Crazy Horse was the leader of the Sioux Nation that defeated General Custer in 1876. This gigantic monument, when completed in 1978, will be 563 feet high and 641 feet long. Ziolkowski comes well-trained for this job. He assisted in the carving of the monuments on Mt. Rushmore. In 18 years, Ziolkowski has almost singlehandedly moved 1,164,000 tons of rock. To complete the job, a total of six million tons of stone will have to be cut from the mountain. The cost of this 30-year operation is being met by funds collected from tourists, private contributors, and Ziolkowski's personal funds.

Mountain-carver **Korczak Ziolkowski** taught himself to carve in wood and to sculpt. His works include a marble head of Paderewski which won a first sculptural award at the New York World's Fair, 1939. He began work on the Crazy Horse Memorial in 1948 and spent most of 1950 and 1951 painting the outline of his proposed monument on the side of Mount Thunderhead.

Singer **Bobby Vinton**

Another Polish-American artist, Wladislaw T. Benda, is noted for his penetrating, imaginative illustrations and his exotic, colorful masks — which are in great demand. Benda's idea for making masks originated when he had to make one for himself to wear to a costume ball.

In the performing arts, Bobby Vinton has earned a name as one of the top young popular singing stars of recent years. His hits, such as "Roses are Red" and "Blue on Blue," have sold millions of copies, even though they did not follow the rock 'n' roll trend. Bobby Vinton had his own band at the age of 15. He has a degree in music from Pittsburgh's Duquesne University.

7. *Sports*

Before 1915, only a few Americans of Polish descent were well-known athletes. Frank Piekarski was a member of the All-American Football Team in 1904, and Stanley Ketchel (Stanislaw Kiecal) won the middleweight boxing title in 1907. Since then, however, there has been a steady stream of sports stars from the Polish ethnic group.

Stan "the Man" Musial is one of the most famous players in the history of baseball and certainly the most famous player of Polish descent. A natural from his high school days, Stan had a difficult

Baseball stars **Stan Musial** and **Carl Yastrzemski**. Musial holds the National League record for hits made, runs batted in, and games played. Yastrzemski, outfielder for the Boston Red Sox, was named Most Valuable Player in the American League for 1967.

time convincing his parents to allow him to play baseball rather than go to college. Musial played outfield and first base for the St. Louis Cardinals from 1941 to 1963. He was voted most valuable player of the National League in 1943, 1946, and 1948. He also won seven National League batting titles. In 1969 Musial was elected to the National Baseball Hall of Fame in Cooperstown, New York.

A much younger, but very impressive figure in baseball is Boston Red Sox outfielder Carl Yastrzemski, who was voted Man of the Year in 1967 by *Sport* magazine. Carl was essential to the Red Sox's surprise victory in the 1967 pennant race.

In college football, All-America honors have been given to one or more Americans of Polish descent almost every year since 1927. In fact, at one point the "Fighting Irish" of Notre Dame had so many Poles on their squad that coach Knute Rockne was asked how he picked his team. "It's a cinch," he answered with a grin. "When I can't pronounce 'em, they're good."

One of the earliest Polish-American football greats was Bronislaw "Bronko" Nagurski. Bronko was an All-America tackle for the University of Minnesota in 1929 and became All-Time National Football League fullback with the Chicago Bears.

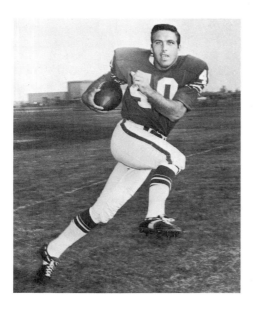

Ed Rutkowski played end for the Buffalo Bills.

Almost every major professional football team in the country has had a player of Polish descent, including Ed Rutkowski of the Buffalo Bills; Mark Smolinski of the New York Jets; Jim Kanicki of the Cleveland Browns; Larry Kaminski of the Denver Broncos; Bob Kowalkowski of the Detroit Lions; and Jim Grabowski of the Green Bay Packers.

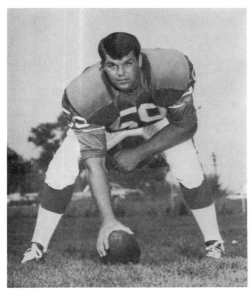

Larry Kaminski, center for the Denver Broncos.

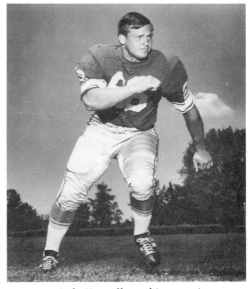

Bob Kowalkowski, guard for the Detroit Lions.

Conclusion

The Poles in America cling tenaciously to their customs, which are in nearly every instance as much religious as they are national in character. They are quick to respond to an appeal to their national or religious sympathies. The Poles love parades, processions, flags, banners, and uniforms. They find that the elaborate and colorful religious celebrations serve to bind them even closer to their church.

Most Polish-Americans observe their national festivals. The month of May recalls the adoption of Poland's Constitution; November, the Revolution of 1830; and January, Poland's insurrection of 1863. In October, the Poles honor the memory of General Casimir Pulaski, and parades in his honor are held in many American cities. In New York, the Pulaski Day Parade is one of the city's largest nationality parades (more than 100,000 Poles participated in 1970). The various Polish organizations vie with one another in preparing these celebrations, which serve to instruct both the younger Polish generation and the people whose own traditions have mingled with those of the Poles in America.

Although only a few of the many outstanding American Poles are mentioned in this volume, there are and were millions of others whose influence and contributions have been felt. As former President Johnson stated on the occasion of the Polish Millenium celebration in 1966, "Our national heritage is rich with the gifts of the Polish people."

...INDEX...

ABOUT THE AUTHOR...

DR. JOSEPH A. WYTRWAL, whose parents trace their ancestry to southern Poland, is a native of Detroit. He received bachelor's and master's degrees from both Wayne State University and the University of Detroit, and his doctorate from the University of Michigan. He has also studied at various universities in the United States and at the University of Warsaw in Poland. Dr. Wytrwal has been a college teacher of English, history, and philosophy. He is currently associated with the Detroit Public Schools and with Endurance Press, which is mainly devoted to publishing journals of Polish interest.

Dr. Wytrwal (pronounced Why-trawl) has written many articles and two other books: *America's Polish Heritage* (1961) and *Poles in American History and Tradition* (1968).

The IN AMERICA *Series*

We specialize in publishing quality books for
young people. For a complete list please write:

LERNER PUBLICATIONS COMPANY
241 First Avenue North, Minneapolis, Minnesota 55401